WHEN LUXURY
WENT TO SEA

WHEN LUXURY WENT TO SEA

Douglas Phillips-Birt

David & Charles : Newton Abbot

ISBN 0 7153 5339 X

Set in 11pt Baskerville
and printed in Great Britain
by W J Holman Limited Dawlish
for David & Charles (Publishers) Limited
South Devon House Newton Abbot Devon

CONTENTS

WHEN LUXURY
WENT TO SEA

The age of the luxury liner opened in the 'nineties of the last century, flared into final brightness in the 'fifties of the present century and lingers smouldering today in the shape of one ship, the French Line's *France*. Meanwhile, another, the Cunard's *QE2*, tries to establish an acceptable modern interpretation of what was once uninhibited, proudly exclusive grandeur afloat.

The liners of this age served the route of gold linking Europe with the brazenly rich United States of America, where a new class of person was learning how to spend money as lavishly as any Old World *rentier*.

'Going Cunard' was then a state of grace, and as the late Lucius Beebe said, 'How You Travelled Was Who You Were'. The liners which provided the means of such travel became curiously loved by many who never saw them: *Olympic, Kaiser Wilhelm der Gross, Mauretania, Imperator, Ile de France, Aquitania, Berengaria, Leviathan, Majestic, Conti di Savoia, Queen Mary*— there is not a name amongst them that suggests other than grandeur or assurance. There was romance, too, in those names, and when the *Mauretania* went to the shipbreaker's yard, people who had never travelled in her felt that a star had fallen into the Atlantic.

These ships, intricate and lavish hotels afloat, were much else besides. They were literally towns afloat, whose quiet Russell Squares you might identify; and their places where the atmosphere had the rich raffishness of the Champs-Elysées in the Junes of the 'nineties. Their steaming alleys and East Sides were never far from where the music and jewels and splendours were to be found, and large though they may have been as ships they were small to carry so much of human contrast, the splendours and the miseries crushed together. Our concern is with the splendours.

In a world where the lot of the seagoer had traditionally been hard, the mere establishment of some degree of comfort on an ocean was a singular achievement. The attainment of luxury could hardly fail to amaze. True that it was a victory of contrivance and could not be continuously successful, since from time to time the sea outside the august dwelling would awkwardly obtrude. Luxury being the voluptuous, the provision of all that is opulent in

7

food, furniture and surroundings, of amenities desirable but not indispensable, the sea is one of the most inconvenient localities in which to establish the milieu; better no doubt than a polar icecap or an over-heated jungle, because more capricious and capable of ineffably gracious moods; but capable too of all that is most inimical to the establishment of even basic comfort.

The boundary between luxury and mere comfort is hard to define, with the added difficulty that in a ship a feature seeming to verge on the luxurious would be taken for granted ashore. Windows, for example, have long been an amenity generally accepted in western society, yet the first ships in which sash windows replaced the former circular portholes seemed luxurious for this reason alone. Previously, only the more highly-paying few had enjoyed in their own cabins casements opening wide on fairy seas, forlorn or otherwise. Luxury at sea was the product of an advancing technology and the greater use of windows afloat was largely due to the discovery that toughened or laminated glass could offer the same strength as twice the thickness of the plate glass which had filled the portholes.

But luxury raised to the level of ostentation was another matter, and the luxury liners were chiefly to the tastes of the middle-aged and elderly in a period when it was not considered delicate to linger overlong beside the fountain of youth.

When Winston Churchill, just twenty-one, crossed from Liverpool to New York in the Cunard's *Etruria* in 1895, he failed to enjoy it. This ship had come into service ten years earlier with the object of capturing the high-priced Atlantic trade. The comfort she offered was considered exceptional, as was the electric light with which she was fitted throughout. She was fast, too—between 1885 and 1888 she and her sister-ship *Umbria* had held the Blue Ribands for east-west and west-east crossings. But while the electric light she burned impressed the passengers and her speed—an average of almost 20 knots—gave her style, the amount of coal she burned appalled her owners. Catering for the rich was costly.

But Winston Churchill was not impressed. 'I do not contemplate ever taking a sea voyage for pleasure and shall always look upon journeys by sea as necessary evils which have to be undergone in the carrying out of any definite plan.' So he wrote to his mother, Lady Randolph Churchill, who had formerly been Jennie Jerome, daughter of Leonard Walter Jerome of New York. Winston Churchill conceded that 'our cabins are not uncomfortable', but the passengers did not satisfy him: 'There are no nice people on board to speak of—certainly none to write of. . . There is to be a concert on board tonight at which all the stupid people among the passengers intend to perform and the stupider ones to applaud. The days have seemed very long and uninteresting.' Some years earlier Winston's father had written unenthusiastically about the amenities of passenger ships, perhaps with more justification than the son (*vide ante*).

8

Noel Coward was once asked in what he found that indefinable something called 'style', and his list—together with a Brixham trawler and a seagull—included what he described as 'evading boredom'. Such has always been the important activity of a tiny section of civilised people, and we might regard the luxury liner as a huge machine devised to assist in the stylish evasion of boredom when travelling. It even made seagoing a pleasure, which would have astounded Dr Johnson.

In the days of the sailing ship, even in its final era and in the largest and most comfortable ships afloat, the idea of seagoing for pleasure was inconceivable. Along that then richest of sea routes, to India, people embarked on the magnificent East Indiamen with little expectation of pleasure and much to encourage apprehension. The best cabins would be no more than 7ft long and 6ft wide, and most of them were formed by canvas screens. In the great cabin aft the hangings might be of rich Indian silks, while the furnishings were a forecast of tomorrow's liners. Food was abundant until it went bad, which would happen early in the voyage; but wines and spirits were plentiful enough and helped to dim the misery of foul drinking water.

There were compensations: such as afternoons on deck in the Indian Ocean, close to where the helmsman stood with an awning like a bell-tent over his head, and passengers drooped in deck chairs under their sunshades with dogs by them stretched out on the hot deck planks. Lord Macaulay, about to set off for India in 1834, was 'assured by all my medical advisors that a week of the sea will make me better than ever I was in my life'. This attitude to a sea voyage must have been splendidly modern in the days when Victoria was still the little princess at Kensington Palace. Of his voyage in an East India-man, Macaulay wrote soon afterwards that nothing occurred to break the monotony of an easy and quick passage: 'The catching of a shark; the shooting of an albatross; a sailor tumbling down a hatchway and breaking his head; a cadet getting drunk and swearing at the captain . . .' were incidents he recalled. As for his fellow passengers, Macaulay was not unhappy to keep apart from them.

Hannah [his sister] will give you histories of all these good people at length, I dare say, for she was extremely social; danced with the gentlemen in the evenings, and read novels and sermons with the ladies in the mornings. I contented myself with being very civil whenever I was with the other passengers, and took care to be with them as little as I could. Except at meals I scarcely exchanged a word with any human being. I never was left for so long a time so completely to my own resources; and I am glad to say I found them quite sufficient to keep me cheerful and employed.

That, however, was Thomas Babington Macaulay, who had ideas enough about how to elude boredom on even a long sea voyage. For most other people, sea travel meant boredom varied with intervals of acute misgiving. Man had not yet learned how to take the sea out of seagoing.

Charles Dickens learned this when he crossed the Atlantic in the Cunard steamship *Britannia* in 1842. Two years earlier the *Britannia* had inaugurated the regular mail and passenger steamship service to America. Leaving Liverpool on the sixty-fourth anniversary of the Declaration of Independence, and watched from the quay by a prosperous crowd, top-hatted and crinolined, waving sticks and handkerchiefs, she made the crossing in twelve days and ten hours—a mere third of the time customary under sail—to receive in Boston as gay and noisy a welcome, with a great banquet for Cunard himself, as can ever have greeted a ship anywhere. Already Cunard was demonstrating beyond question that the future of transatlantic navigation lay with steam, despite such objections as that of Dr Larder, who had recently declared: 'Steam on the North Atlantic is merely a dream; and as to any idiotic project of making the voyage direct from Liverpool to New York under steam, I have no hesitation in saying that one might as well talk of making such a voyage from here to the moon'. The *Britannia* marked the opening of the era which was to lead to the age of luxury, but it was some way off as yet.

The *Britannia* was 207ft in length, with a gross tonnage of 1,154. Fifty years later a ship three times her length and twelve times her tonnage was to personify the most exuberant lavishness yet set afloat.

Meanwhile, Cunard's agent in London was doing his best for the *Britannia*, which indeed offered an impressive combination of speed and comfort, the speed no doubt seeming particularly attractive to those whose main objection to ocean voyaging was the long and unpredictable time taken, with the consequent prolongation of ennui or worse. Dickens was shown pictures of *Britannia's* staterooms, 'chaste and pretty, not to say gorgeous little bowers', and of the main saloon, 'a chamber of almost interminable perspective furnished . . . in a style of more than Eastern splendour, and filled (but not inconveniently so) with groups of ladies and gentlemen, in the very highest state of enjoyment and vivacity'.

But going on board for the first time he found himself faced with a cabin which was to him 'a profoundly preposterous box'. But he comforted himself with the possibility that 'this room of state' was a 'cheerful jest of the captain's invented and put into practice for the better relish and enjoyment of the real stateroom presently to be disclosed. . .'

But no, alas, this really was his cabin, 'with the two berths, one above the other, than which nothing smaller for sleeping in was ever made except coffins'. And he quickly discovered what was basic to all ships' accommodation arrangements at that time:

> There was the stewardess, too, actively engaged in producing clean sheets and tablecloths from the very entrails of the sofas, and from unexpected lockers, of such artful mechanism, that it made one's head ache to see them opened one after another . . . to find every nook and corner and individual piece of furniture as something else besides what it pretended to be, and was a mere trap and deception and place of secret stowage. . .

And the saloon, at the level of the main deck, disquieted him no less. Instead of Eastern splendour, he faced

> ...a long narrow apartment, not unlike a gigantic hearse with windows in the sides; having at the upper end a melancholy stove, at which three or four chilly stewards were warming their hands; while on either side extending down the whole dreary length, was a long, long table, over each of which a rack, fixed to the low roof, and stuck full of drinking glasses and cruet stands, hinted dismally at rolling seas and heavy weather.

Dickens' account of the meals on this early Cunarder is in striking contrast to the cuisine to appear in later Atlantic liners, planned by master chefs and prepared by cooks numbering between fifty and a hundred. He watched the stores being shipped.

> ...one party of men were 'taking in the milk', or, in other words, getting the cow on board; and another was filling the icehouses to the very throat with fresh provisions; with butchers' meat and gardenstuff, pale sucking-pigs, calves' heads in scores, beer, veal and pork, and poultry out of all proportion...

During the days at sea, the bell for luncheon would be rung at one o'clock, and in would come the stewardess with steaming plates of baked potatoes and roasted apples, another steaming dish of hot collops, and an array of cold dishes—salt beef, cold ham, pig's face. The next meal came at five o'clock, with boiled potatoes this time, various hot meats, and especially the

> ...roast pig, to be taken medically. We sit down at table again...prolong the meal with a rather mouldy dessert of apples, grapes and oranges; and drink our wine and brandy-and-water. The bottles and glasses are still upon the table, and the oranges and so forth are rolling about according to their fancy and the ship's way, when the doctor comes down, by special nightly invitation, to join our evening rubber...

The spirit of ennui lay heavily over the first-class passengers' accommodation, and perhaps still more heavily and hopelessly over the packed steerage which Dickens was not allowed to visit. In her saloon and staterooms the *Britannia* carried a few suffering passengers, while crammed elsewhere in the traditional fashion of the steerage were a vast quantity more. The less uncomfortable passengers read, when they could find a seat where it was light enough, or dozed between spasms of bored talk. Dickens made his first passage in bad weather, though perhaps it was not as severe as he made it out to be in his disgust at having to drink brandy-and-water and eat hard biscuit. 'And so she goes on staggering, heaving, wrestling, leaping, diving, jumping, pitching, throbbing, rolling, and rocking; and going through all these movements, sometimes by turns, and sometimes altogether; until one feels disposed to roar for mercy.' A steward described the conditions as a rather heavy sea and a head wind; the captain regularly told the passengers it would be better tomorrow, to which Dickens acidly observed that apparently at sea it always is going to be better tomorrow.

Some twenty years had to pass after Dickens' voyage before the *Great Eastern* staggered her generation. She did not belong to the age of luxurious seagoing, but she anticipated it, along with much else, in her size, which was not surpassed until the *Lusitania*, firmly implanted in the age of luxury, went into service almost half a century later.

The future spoke in the *Great Eastern's* 'Grand Saloon', the first of many grander saloons just round the corner of the years. While small compared with what was to be put afloat by the next generation, its length of 63ft, breadth of 47ft, and its height of 14ft—modest compared with future saloons rising through three decks—were more than enough to amaze. A balcony ran each side of the saloon supported on slim pillars, proud evidence of how effectively the nineteenth-century creative engineer could use iron. A delicate iron balustrade surrounded the balcony. Period decoration had not yet gone afloat.

The walls were hung with rich stuffs heavily patterned, the *portieres* on the doorways were of crimson velvet, and the floor was deeply carpeted. Everything in the room was reflected and reflected again in mirrors on four sides of the funnel casings, which pierced the saloon in their plunge to the boilers; and all was repeated again in the mirrors on the air shafts. Pilasters imitated oxidised silver, and overhead were immense gilded and convoluted chandeliers carrying the gas lighting. Everything, for the first time in a ship, was larger than life.

The appointments in the first-class cabins were to be admired. Each cabin contained a wash-basin, dressing-table and rocking-chair, as well as berths, and the presence of a bath with running hot and cold water was compensation enough for it being hidden away under one of the berths. The latter were not immune from criticism, however, and a young lady, illustrated in lithographs published at the time of the ship's maiden voyage, had her objections reported in the captions:

> My berth is the uppermost one, and I have to climb up to it, putting one foot on the lower one, and the other way out, which is a great stretch and makes it very straining—then I lift one knee on the berth, and roll in sideways. Last night I put my foot on Mrs. Brown's face as she lay asleep close to the edge of the lower one, and nearly put her eye out.
>
> To dismount is another feat of horsemanship only fit for a sailor. You can't sit up for the floor overhead so you have to turn round, and roll your legs out first and then hold on till you touch bottom somewhere, and then let yourself down upright. It is dreadful work and not very decent for a delicate female, if the steward happens to come in when you are in the act this way.

Later, but still prior to the age of North Atlantic luxury, Lord Randolph Churchill travelled to the East in a steamship belonging to a then well-known company and recorded his impressions in a series of articles for an English journal. Among much else that was critical, he described the food and drink on board as like that of a second-rate lodging house. When he was attacked in

12

the press for his opinion, one of his supporters averred that the merchant service had become Britain's sacred cow, and that a little criticism for a change might do the service some good. The disreputable but perceptive Frank Harris wrote of this episode:

> All the mercantile world, whose patriotism is mainly self-interest, and their champions in the press, kept on ridiculing him [Lord Randolph] month in month out till they had seriously damaged his reputation with the many. Yet food on board ship was bad everywhere till Ballin lifted all ocean travel into a higher category of comfort. He was the first to make sea life luxurious.

Despite Lord Randolph Churchill, those passenger ships of modest size which maintained the communications of Empire were, in fact, offering steadily-improving standards of seaborne well-being, which would certainly have pleased Dickens.

These were the days of the 'P & O Pencillings', line drawings of life on board; and Harry Furness took time away from his brilliant cartoons of political figures to make sketches of deck scenes in the ships bound to the Far East. 'Pyjama Parade 7 am' is the caption of one, showing decks being hosed down by Asiatic deck hands while the Empire Builders, no doubt happy to leave their small staterooms to their early-rising wives, paddled around with bare feet in their night attire. Another scene, entitled with arch-humour 'A Red Sea-iesta', is a truly horrible spectacle of sleepers in deck chairs packed close in an awning-covered space.

To help passengers keep fit, there were deck sports, though only for the men. They struggled through bottomless barrels suspended aloft, splashed over water jumps arranged in canvas tarpaulins, and engaged in a game known as 'cock-fighting'. Or in the more reverential frame of mind appropriate to the game, the products of the major and minor public schools played cricket on a tiny pitch in a netted-in space of deck.

Duty done and health assured, there were music rooms with draped pianos and draped seats, where the invigorated Anglo-Indian males bent with sheets of music over the no less well-draped ladies. There were smoking-rooms with fewer frills, where men with pipes spoke with men smoking cigars, and during evenings in the saloon, its heavy panelling pierced with little curtained portholes, chess and backgammon would be played, watched perhaps by a bearded and benevolent ship's officer. The staterooms to which they all eventually retired sought to divert attention from the evident pressure of their two coffin-width berths, one closely above the other, by a lavish display on the dressing tables before which the ladies' maids had pinned in their mistresses for dinner. But the dressing tables were half-hearted affairs, and just over them would be folded down, when essential but never convenient, the two washbasins. After use, those would be tipped up again to send the water cascading in a soapy flurry down into the waste tank.

Three times a day the ship's bugler called the passengers to meals: breakfast, tiffin and dinner. Three times a day the bugler paraded round the alleys and corridors and up and down the companionways which, with the growing sophistication of ship interiors, were now beginning to look more like what most passengers called them—staircases—fairly wide and with handsomely carved balusters. In the dining saloon were the ranks of long tables, rather like a dining-room at school but scattered with hand-written menus, perhaps thirty Anglo-Saxon items long. Sometimes the ominous fiddles criss-crossed the tables, over which, when the Western Ocean swell came into the Bay of Biscay, the plates would jump and the bottles fall, while everyone around the board became determinedly amusing to show that they could bear it, and even enjoy an apple turnover (middle of the last course) at the same time.

Then, after so many weeks, during which coteries would have been formed and some intense attachments made which must never, oh! *never*, be forgotten! the luggage would be up on deck—little stacks expressive of the caravanserai and all that is fleeting—and the voyage would be over.

The life on board such ships was friendly, if perhaps a little aggressively team-spirited, cosy, well-mannered, *gemutlich*. But it was not smart, for these were the ships of the sons bound to exile in order to serve, as their poet told them, their captives' need—the new caught sullen peoples, the fluttered folk and wild. But over on the other side of a less sunny ocean was a land where something else was fluttering. It was a land which, in the eyes of quite well informed people, seemed to be densely populated with heiresses, mostly intent on getting to Paris. Their families came too. From yonder where, according to another poet, came flooding in the main, and flood and reflux crossed the Atlantic as the Old World discovered the Great Republic, and the Republic rediscovered the Old in the persons of thousands of Daisy Millers, their brothers and aunts and mamas and couriers. Their papas did not come along so often, being occupied with their Trusts. But they paid. And the North Atlantic route, the already old 'Atlantic Ferry', became a route of gold.

The Americans, whom Professor David Potter had described as the 'people of plenty', moving inland from the east and west coasts, had some time earlier met in the middle, and now were spread over the millions of square miles of peerless opportunity which was the United States. Following the covered waggon times—the era of settlement and agriculture—had come the growth of the great business corporations. The day arrived when it happened that one corporation—United States Steel—owned the whole steel wealth of the sub-continent and while more men than ever before were becoming rich, some were becoming richer than men had ever been. There appeared more gold labels on more cut-glass decanters, tended by excellent butlers trained elsewhere, and the Rolls-Royce of the Old World and the size of cigar proudly symbolised the new achievements. There was a widespread conviction that all this was as it should be—had not John D. Rockefeller told a Sunday school

14

that it was according to the laws of God and nature? The workings of the law were personified by Rockefeller himself, by the Frisks, Mellons, Whitneys, Carnegies, and Morgans; by Mrs G. Gould's $500,000 necklace, and by the slightly less costly necklaces belonging to the wives of thousands of lesser Goulds. But it was significant that in that rich, *parvenu* society, the Goulds for a long time were not quite acceptable. The frame of mind that was to prefer the private suites of the great liners soon to appear was in process of being formed.

It was in 1895 that Consuelo Vanderbilt, who had just become the new and very young Duchess of Marlborough, voyaged over the Atlantic to her new home. 'Crossing the Atlantic in those days,' she wrote later (1953), 'was not the luxurious affair it is now. Ships were much smaller and there were no beautifully decorated suites, no Ritz restaurant, no cinema and no radio.' She wrote with some experience of ships. Her family had made part of their fortune in shipping. In the childhood she was leaving behind she had known her father's 2,000 ton yacht *Valiant*. She had heard of her great-grandfather's *North Star*, 'the largest yacht that had even been constructed for a pleasure voyage', she said.

At first it was the speed of the new ships on the North Atlantic route and their ability to adhere to schedules that gripped the public's imagination. Passages on the sailing ships had been of unpredictable duration, and it was an achievement in keeping with an age conscious of its progress and material success that ships could now cross the Western Ocean dependably and rapidly. In a sitting-room of the Carlton Hotel in London the breathless traveller might exclaim with wonder, over the first cup of English tea served by an old world servant in breeches, 'Just to think that six *days* ago I was in Manhattan!' To be in London today six hours after leaving New York by air is no more cause for wonder than was that miracle of a six-day sea passage to an earlier generation. Then, as now, speed was fashionable and had sales value and since, for technical reasons, higher speeds at sea meant larger ships, so their size grew. And with size came the opportunity to provide the lavish appointments so agreeable to those whose social aspirations depended so much upon appearances.

In 1900 the *Kaiser Wilhelm der Grosse*, owned by the Norddeutscher Lloyd, was the fastest liner afloat, having just outpaced the four Cunard ships which were maintaining that line's New York services.

Another German line—known, when you were not in a hurry, as the Hamburg Amerikanische Packetfahrt Actiengesellschaft, or more conveniently, the Hamburg-Amerika line—which was shortly to institute an era of unparalleled luxury afloat, produced a vessel that outsped the *Kaiser Wilhelm der Grosse*. This was the *Deutschland*. While the *Kaiser Wilhelm der Grosse* had taken 5 days, 22 hours and 45 minutes between the Needles and Sandy Hook, the *Deutschland* cut 6½ hours from the passage by going a knot faster. This was an achievement of one kind, but the faster ship never became as popular as the one she defeated. Her engines, of one-fifth more horsepower, produced vibration that even a speed-loving clientele preferred to do without, while she voraciously ate her coal supply and profits as she went.

Both ships were strikingly handsome, their four tall funnels grouped in pairs, with masts and funnels raked to the lines of speed. Four funnels were vital status symbols then, and those who voyaged beneath fewer were keeping suspect company. The Norddeutscher Lloyd replied to the *Deutschland* with the *Kronprinz Wilhelm*, which in turn proved the faster ship. She was followed by the *Kaiser Wilhelm II*, another record-breaker which gained the Blue Riband of the Atlantic; but it was already becoming apparent that the cost of gaining this coveted distinction outweighed any commercial advantage, and by this time the Hamburg-Amerika line had given up the record-breaking business. Indeed, the *Deutschland* was the only very fast ship ever built for the line. With Albert Ballin in charge of the Hamburg-Amerika line, new ideas began to prevail. The age of luxury at sea had arrived, and this German-Jewish shipowner became the first man to establish magnificence afloat in the largest possible ships.

Speed was of secondary importance. Ballin sought to make the transatlantic passage so comfortable that the longer voyage—longer by perhaps a day—would be looked upon as an advantage. Seagoing was to become a delight to be lingered over. Against the express liners—*schnelldampfer*—he opposed the slower, bigger *postdampfer*. Dr Wiegand of the rival Norddeutscher Lloyd line continued to believe in express liners, and so too did the Cunard line, which was encouraged by a state loan of £2¼ million to build two ships, the *Mauretania* and the *Lusitania*, fast and fuel-hungry enough to require a subsidy to keep them running without putting their owners out of business. With these ships, the average speed across the Atlantic leapt from the 22 knots of the *Deutschland* to some 26 knots.

Though the White Star Line had toyed with the idea of high speed, they finally decided, like Ballin, to come down on the side of high living, and settled on a policy of building large ships of moderate speed. Their answer to Cunard's *Mauretania* and *Lusitania* was the *Olympic* and the *Titanic*, and the contrast between the two pairs of ships was a measure of the difference between the philosophies which had inspired them. The *Olympic* and *Titanic* were about half as big again as the *Mauretania* and the *Lusitania* in terms of gross tonnage, but the latter had half as much power again as the White Star's pair, enabling them to shorten the time of crossing by about one day. But, as the Hamburg-Amerika and the White Star lines argued, their ships could offer that extra day in which to enjoy such luxury as had never before been set afloat.

For Ballin's Hamburg-Amerika Line, the great lavish ships followed one another—the *Kaiserin Auguste Victoria* after the *Amerika* in 1906, the

16

Imperator in 1913, the yet larger *Vaterland* in 1914, and, still on the building slip in that year when the old world dissolved, the *Bismarck*. Under names redolent of old imperialisms the ships made money out of the plutocracy of a new world republic which spurned arms and armour and aristocracy, though about the last its attitude was at least ambivalent. In the new world which eventually dragged itself out of the shambles, these ships reappeared under names still remembered by some: the *Vaterland* as the American *Leviathan*, the *Imperator* as the Cunard's *Berengaria*, the *Bismarck* as the White Star's *Majestic*—names less imperious, but still rich in dominion. And other ships of similar character were with them: the *Aquitania*, to be joined by the *Normandie*, the *Bremen*, and the *Queen Mary*, followed by yet others, which were still running along that route of gold when the stream feeding it faltered and eventually dried under the roar of jet engines.

Products of a society whose besetting vulgarity was ostentation, liners of the age when luxury was at its most exuberant would no doubt appear shocking to modern tastes. But today's liners, as they struggle to meet egalitarian responses better suited to supersonic capsules, would no less ruffle the susceptabilities of those who found their ease among the furbelows of yesterday. What would those ladies in discreet draperies have said about their successors today, sprawling leggily among the plastics after a brisk spell of athletics on the games deck? Ships are able to parody tastes by the concentration of their effects, and yesterday's ships effectively parodied those of Victorian and Edwardian England and Wilhelmine Germany. It was not so much that discomfort had been banished—that could still intrude, even though well-cushioned, in a North Atlantic winter—but rather was it the fact that the height of opulence had been set afloat. The ships were period pieces, they were Charlottenburg Palace, the Gothic Chatsworth; they were all the Ritz hotels of the western world with more than a touch of San Francisco's Palace Hotel thrown in, amazingly established on the sea. Inevitably, they were described as 'floating cities'. A captain of the Cunard line could not avoid the cliché: '*Aquitania*, 1,500 miles west Bishop's Rock. In that short line is contained a fairy tale come true—the fairy tale of a city that floats in mid-Atlantic.'

And not only was it a city to the extent of its stratified population and social extremes; it was also a capital city. There were the Grosvenor Squares, the Faubourgs Saint Germain, and not a little of what caused some people to describe the Berlin of the day as 'Parvenupopolis'. That gilded eagle, with an imperial crown perched as if by accident on its feathered head, which projected from the bow of the *Imperator*, was the perfect symbol of an attitude. Symbolic too, perhaps, was the fact that the Atlantic carried it away on the ship's third voyage—eagle, crown, and the globe across which was written, beneath the scrabbling claws, *Mein Feld Ist Die Welt*.

The floating cities had their graduations from 1st class through the 2nd to the plain discomfort of the 3rd, below which might be the courts and alleys of the steerage and the bridges under which the numerous crew lived. At the maximum there might have been 700 first-class passengers on board; nearly 4,000 more would be in the third class and steerage and amongst the crew; and of the crew, two-thirds would be stewards and domestic staff—600-700 in the largest ships. In contrast, the deck and engine-rooms would be manned, and the ship operated as a reliable seagoing machine, by a mere 200 men. Two hundred, amongst perhaps 5,000, were enough to turn 'the fairy tale of the city that floats in mid-Atlantic' into a fully functioning ship that regularly, according to timetable, would pass down, perhaps, the S-channel from Southampton docks, swing round close to the shore of the Isle of Wight, and out towards the Atlantic by way of Spithead and its forts. Then, with the great vessel pointing steadily westward towards the finger piers of New York, the concerts and the rich meals, the theatre shows and parties, private and public, would begin, and for long periods the soft throb of turbines far below heedless feet would be the only reminder that it was all happening on the disconcerting sea.

Everything in the environment of the first-class passengers sought to deny the existence of the sea, though the period furnishings so familiar on shore were apt to take upon themselves a disconcerting unreality when all the surroundings of plinth and column, capital and pediment rose, swayed and fell to the seas, and the great open spaces were criss-crossed by ropes of horribly nautical aspect to serve as hand rails.

Luxury went to sea in the 'nineties accompanied by period furnishing because it was a mechanic age in which only the engineer worked with confidence, and the beauty latent in the machine had yet to be released. In former times passenger ships had usually been designed internally, as in all else, by the shipyards, where no Adam or Chippendale was employed. The heavy furnishings that resulted, probably in bird's eye maple and deep red mahogany monstrously shaped, were redeemed by strength and fine craftsmanship; above all by appropriateness to the seagoing function. But they could not excite, and their marine adequacy could certainly not entice those to whom the sea was something to be passed over as heedlessly as might be contrived.

In the absence of imagination, the creations that genius had once raised on land out of stone were adapted to cover, in imitations of that stone, what the genius of modern engineering had created in pliable, adventurous steel. Also pressed into service were a variety of other methods of disguising the metals that were the real triumph of the time.

So the *Aquitania*, which first went into service briefly in 1914, had a Caroline smoking room, an Elizabethan grill room, a Louis XIV dining room and a Palladian lounge, while the swimming pool was inspired by Egyptian remains in the British Museum and flanked by fluted columns of dubious origin. Disguise became the driving principle behind the furnishing.

18

Without question, the *Aquitania* was one of the most comfortable and popular liners afloat for several decades. Yet even some of those most devoted to the ship questioned the appropriateness of what a distressing *jeu d'esprit* sometimes called 'the principal inn of the city'—complete with oak beamed ceiling and leaded windows. 'Period' was a style that died hard afloat, and when in the early 'thirties two new Italian liners, the *Rex* and the *Conte di Savoia*, came into service, their mainly contemporary style of decoration was a welcome example of the visual awareness that is the gift of that nation's designers. Even so, the most striking feature of the *Conte di Savoia* internally was the Grand Colonna Hall by Gustavo Pulitzer Finali of Trieste, which took its name from the gallery of the seventeenth-century Collonia Palace in Rome, dating from 1620. The nave of the huge apartment, whose ceiling soared 24ft high, carried a reproduction of Lucchesini's painting of the battle of Lepanto in the Collonia gallery, and was flanked by marble pilasters with friezes and cornices in the seventeenth-century manner. In the two wide aisles stood reproductions of classical sculpture and space was used with splendid extravagance to express all the luxury that had ever gone to sea or ever would.

It is easy to object to the tastes of a few generations past; they were what they were partly because contemporary design had failed to discover any new and satisfying idioms. But no sympathy can reach to the great staircase in the *Titanic*, which had at its head bronze figures said to represent Honour and Glory, when anyone who gave them passing thought would have recognised them as Acquisition and Avarice.

If 'How you travelled was who you were', and 'Going Cunard was a state of grace', then it was aspiring to the steps of the throne itself when a traveller could afford to disregard the magnificence of the first-class rooms and travel high in his own set of self-contained and sumptuously-appointed apartments, consisting of a large sitting-room, bedrooms, bathrooms, dressing-room, trunk room and private verandah. Totally insulated for six days if they wished, and never setting foot in a public part of the ship, such travellers were a whisper only amongst mere first-class passengers. Occasionally the whisper would become personified, and a figure, or several belonging to that charmed circle apart, would be seen on their verandah on the sunny side of the ship—starboard side when Old World bound, port side for the return—looking over the sea or down on the promenade decks, common ground as seen from the verandah but each dauntingly forbidden fruit to those treading the planks of the decks belonging to the next lower class. Then they would disappear to their own rooms, less splendid than the nearby saloons, but the essence of discreet luxury.

The style lay in the aloofness. It was the reverse of what Beebe has described as 'the infamies of mass transport of hundreds of passengers jammed into day-coach accommodation in a supersonic cartridge for delivery in London or Paris in a few hours...' These rented luxury flats afloat were the marine counterpart of that greatest of American success symbols on shore, the private railroad car, though even White Star and Cunard could not rise to the gold-plated plumbing on one such privately-owned wagon, or the sybaritic arrangement in another by which, at the mere touch of a button, a partition separating the beds in two adjacent staterooms was most conveniently made to disappear. Neither before nor since has transcontinental travel ever been raised to such an acme of cushioned ease as that made possible by the private railroad car in combination with the private suite in a liner. Thus a traveller might move from San Francisco to Southampton, carried smoothly across a continent of toil and rugged adventure in a pullman of many rooms and comfort towards a seagoing suite, in which he would move with fine confidence over an ocean that might seem to have been trained and tamed merely to provide the traveller's exquisite way.

The finest pullman car might cost a third of a million dollars. Merely to rent a liner's private suite for five days, and so escape the more exuberant ostentations of the first-class accommodation, cost in 1910 rather more than £850 on top of the ordinary fare.

Private suites continued to be in demand and reached something like a glorious climax in the French Line's *Normandie*, which went into service in 1935. This vessel, with her three enormous funnels and smooth external lines which swept with Gallic aplomb from bow to stern of the largest hull ever to have been set afloat, made her British rival, the *Queen Mary*, appear a little fussed and dowdy, a little too sullenly conventional. This longest of ships had also the biggest room ever to have been built into a ship, the Grand Dining Room more than 300ft long and above five times the length of the *Great Eastern's* Grand Saloon which had made early Victorians wonder. The Grand Dining Saloon was panelled in moulded glass tiles illuminated from behind, and from the main room heavy bronze doors opened onto eight smaller dining rooms.

There were two dozen cabins with private verandahs some 5yd by 3yd in extent, and each suite had its individual decorative scheme. There were also ten *suites de luxe* and four *suites de grande luxe*, the latter having dining rooms as well as sitting rooms, so enabling passengers who had paid the price for travelling in a ship with such a Grand Dining Room to avoid having to use it. Two of the *grande luxe* suites, named 'Deauville' and 'Trouville', had no mere verandahs, but private decks situated right aft on terraced areas which looked over the stern, each private deck being 45ft by 16ft.

In the early 'thirties the sister ships *Manhattan* and *Washington* were the most impressive ships of the United States Lines, but they indicated the shape of things to come in being cabin-class ships, with less emphasis on *la grande luxe*. They attempted the difficult feat of providing luxury at moderate prices, but their twelve suites were not unworthy of the route of gold, for each had its own sitting-room, bedroom, foyer and large bathroom plumbed in the best transatlantic manner. Sydney Howard has written of them:

> The decorations of the suites are distinctive. The Monticello and Fairfax suites are modelled on Southern Colonial lines. Louis XVI decorations characterise the Marie Antoinette and Trianon suits. The Devon and Stratford suites are in the Adam style and the Marquette and Frontenac suites in the French provincial style. Two early English suites, Hampton and Rushbrook, and two in later English style, Kensington and Pembroke, complete the number. All are finished in polished hardwood panelling or painted panels.

There was still a good deal of 'period' even in these ships. The library was Elizabethan, the writing room Hepplewhite, and the two-decks-high main saloon was Georgian. On the promenade deck aft, there was a café in the Venetian manner and a smoking-room with log fires, rich in the pioneering spirit with Redskins painted on the walls by Lazzarini.

Sometimes those in the private suites would find themselves eating with others at the captain's table in the first-class dining-room. No other maritime custom so clearly reveals the mystique surrounding a ship's command as this convention giving an often coveted social distinction to those who shared the captain's board. Plain man of the sea he might be, a suburban home behind him run by a wife who was a stranger to smartness. But something of the latter quality was liable to become rubbed off on the ships' officers who climbed through the ranks of the mail ships and reached command. They could adapt to a different world, and some came to enjoy the stately amenities and grave steps in the social dance which was swaying into its last movement. Thus, while the ice drew nearer over the Grand Banks, Captain E. J. Smith, dinner over in the *Titanic*, sat at table with people not only the social writers might describe as rich and famous, enjoying a second cigar, and surrounded by flowers tended by the ship's gardener. Some miles away, dinner that night would have been over for Captain Arthur Rostron (not yet knighted) of the *Carpathia*, who tomorrow would be rushing his ship towards New York with the few survivors from the *Titanic* on board. Captain Rostron did not bring to the diners at his table the lightness of touch that satisfies the worldling, or the bluff bonhomie that some landsmen used to believe was native to seamen.

A world war had taken a scythe to the styles admired before 1914, and the age of debunking was in full swing when Julia, in Evelyn Waugh's novel *Brideshead Revisited*, says to her husband as the liner leaves New York, 'Let's go to dinner. We're at the Captain's table. I don't suppose he'll be down tonight, but it's polite to be fairly punctual.'

So Julia spoke in the voice of her parents. It was different later in the voyage. ' "Saw you two last night at the Captain's table," another passenger said, "with all the nobs".'

' "Very dull nobs",' was Julia's husband's reply. The voyage proceeded and a gale passed. 'That night the captain dined at his table and the circle was complete... The captain was full of chaff at Julia's endurance in the storm, offering to engage her as a seaman; years of seagoing had given him jokes for every occasion.'

It was Sir James Charles, latterly Commodore of the Cunard Line, who in earlier days established the grand manner in captain's hospitality. 'Guests at Sir James's table lived by protocol,' Lucius Beebe has written.

> It was an age when the dinner jacket was not in universal acceptance among Englishmen as evening attire, and one's steward, on instructions from the bridge, laid out smoking or tails as the commodore might have decreed and left a note naming the dinner hour. You didn't dine at your convenience but the Commodore's and on evening's of the Captain's Dinner full evening dress was required with decorations, which put Americans, unless they were of military background, at a disadvantage in the matter of crosses, ribbons and miniatures.
>
> Sir James's tastes at table were vaguely those of Emil Jannings playing Henry VIII. Stewards rolled in carcasses of whole roasted oxen one night, and the next evening small herds of grilled antelope surrounded a hilltop of Strasbourg *foie gras* surmounted by peacock fans. Electrically-illuminated *pieces montées* representing the Battle of Waterloo and other patriotic moments made an appearance while the ship's orchestra played Elgar. Chefs in two-foot-high hats emerged to make thrusts in tierce at turrets of Black Angus beef that towered above the arched eyebrows of the diners, soufflés the size of the chefs' hats blossomed towards the end, like the final set pieces of a Paine's fireworks display on the Fourth of July. Throughout these flanking movements and skirmishes champagne circulated in jeroboams, Mumm's 1916, Irroy, and Perrier-Jouet...

On such evenings a magnifico of the sea was able to encounter, with no less flamboyance but rather more style, the plutocrats of Pittsburgh.

These were the days when Ritz and Escoffier, with the fine food served in their restaurants, could draw out even those who would not otherwise have eaten publicly. Ritz produced his famous design of dining-room, the Adam-styled oval room down whose broad, shallow staircase every entry became a little drama, and similar rooms were built into the Hamburg-Amerika liners, and followed by others. Charles Scotto, a favourite pupil of Escoffier, became chef in the liner *Amerika*, and Escoffier himself was on board to supervise a banquet for the Kaiser. Later he was also in charge of the imperial kitchens of the *Imperator* when the Kaiser spent some time on board.

In the P & O ships, in contrast, the menus were of resounding Englishness. Thus, in the ss *Simla* on 15 January 1862, there was a choice in the first course of the following roasts: turkey, sucking pig, goose, duck, fowl, beef, and two kinds of mutton. There was also boiled beef, boiled mutton and boiled fowl, curried beef and corned beef, pigs' feet stewed, sheep's head braised, kidney pudding, kidney curry and rice. The sole contribution from the cuisine of France was chicken sauté. Has not Prosper Montagne said in his splendid *Larousse Gastronomique* 'The essence of English cookery lies in choosing ingredients of the finest quality and cooking them so that their flavour and texture are fully developed with the minimum addition of ingredients to mask the fine natural taste of the original food?'

For the second course, there followed an array of puddings as English as a

Cornish lane, however much they might raise eyebrows in the nation that guides western gastronomy: fruit tarts, Black Cap pudding, sandwich pastry, baked custard, apple turnover, sponge cake, jam tartlets, Brighton rocks, pancakes. There was also rice pudding.

It was not for such fare that the plutocrats left Pittsburg during the bonanza years, nor that on which the forbiddingly rich in Massachusetts expected to be sustained as they transferred themselves at intervals to the Ritz hotels of the European capitals. And it must be confessed that one needs to be very English or very hungry to blame them. The way to the epicurian heights at sea was not taken in a single step. On a June day in 1891, on board the Norddeutscher Lloyd express liner *Ravel*, the following was offered on menus attractively illustrated with coloured sketches and tinted silhouettes, printed in Gothic German and English:

Dinner
Oxtail soup
Ragout in shells
Roast venison with string beans
Fillet slices with asparagus
Sweetbreads in aspic with sauce remoulade
Roast chicken
Compôt   Salad
Orange pudding
Tranrp. ice   Almond tart
Fruit   Dessert
Coffee

But there was still some way to rise to the gastronomic glories of the first-class menu on board the *Aquitania* in later years—the *Aquitania* in which Sir James Charles presided at the head of his table:

Carte du Jour
DINNER

To Order:
HORS D'ŒUVRES

Grapefruit au Maraschino	Honey Dew Melon
Oysters on Half-Shell	Caviare
Clam Juice Cocktails	Tomate Vinaigrette
Œufs farcis	Anchovy Salad
Andouille de Vire	Antipasta
Smoked Salmon Olives	Pickled Tunny Fish
Smoked Sardines	Gendarme Herrings
Salami and Liver Sausage	Smoked Sturgeon
Salted Peanuts	Westphalia Ham
Salted Almonds	Salted Cucumber

SOUPS

Poule au Pot Henri IV	Potage Dauphine
Consommé Italienne	Potage Stamboul
Consommé Grimaldi	Soup Beaucaire

FISH

Turbot poché Sauce Fenouil Eperlans frits Ravigote
Suprême de Britt Portugaise
Rouget grillé Beurre Diable

23

ENTREES

Noisettes d'Agneau Maltaise   Ris de Veau Osielle
Côtelettes de Volaille aux Haricots Panachées
Pigeonneaux en Cocotte Paysanne   Bouchées Financiére
Escallops de Homard Bellevue

GRILLS

Entrecôte Minute   French Lamb Chops
Calf's Liver Diable   Port Cutlets - Piquante

JOINTS

Prime Sirloins and Ribs of Beef - Horseradish Sauce
Saddle of English Mutton - Red Currant Jelly

ROASTS

Turkey   Pheasant   Guinea Chicken
Quails   Woodcock   Rouen Duck

VEGETABLES

Haricots Verts   Chouxfleur sauté
Vegetable Marrow au Beurre   Fried Oyster Plant
Potatoes - Boiled   New   Roast   Purée
Parmentier   Candied Sweet   Saratoga   Fried

SALADS

Laitue   Tomates   Céléri
de Légumes   Belgian Endive   Combination
Florida French, Roquefort, Lemon & Russian Dressing

ENTREMETS

Pouding Gastronomé   Baked Vanilla Custard
Crêpes Aquitania   Petits Fours
Macedoine de Fruits au Liqueur   Pâtisserie Française

ICES

Vanilla   Peach   Coupes Mary Garden
Melon Water Ice   Neapolitaine

SAVOURIES

Canapé Wheeler   Diable à Cheval   Canapé Quo Vadis
Croûtes au Fromage   Pailles au Parmesan

DESSERT

Apples   Oranges   Tangerines
Grapes   Pears   Bananas

Coffee

It was sometimes necessary to shatter the exact French of the cuisine if the first-class passengers of several nationalities, and assumed inadequacy in any but their mother tongue, were to be sure of what they were being offered. Efforts to combine comprehensibility with chic had some startling results, as in another first-class menu in the *Aquitania*. Amongst the 'Ready Dishes' for dinner, the English (and Americans) had to accept 'Saddle *de* English Mutton', while the French, and those who had risen to the French of the cuisine, found themselves faced with 'Ris *of* Veau, Osielle'. The menu proceeded in a more happily bilingual way with 'Chouxfleur Saute, Haricots Verts and Potatoes Various'. The last were perhaps offerings much better than they sound. The purest French reigns later in 'Macedoine de Fruits au Liqueur', but might be regarded as fractured again in 'Coupes Mary Garden'. The French, who do not quite approve of savouries, were perhaps puzzled over the offering of 'Diable à Cheval'.

As Captain E. G. Diggle and officials of the Cunard Line, who in the 'thirties collaborated to produce the book *The Romance of a Modern Liner*,

24

pointed out:

> Preparing the menus alone is an extremely complicated business. The millionaire type of passnger is naturally very particular, not only about the quality but also the variety of dishes... Of course, not all classes on board expect to dine in a style equal to that of the first-class passengers... althoughly precisely the same food (with per-haps lesser variety) is cooked under the same conditions.

In the third class of those days, now nearly half a century ago, the broth was Scotch, the onions creamed and the potatoes frankly browned. Also the cabbage was 'spring'. There were pickles, and as well as coffee at the end there was iced tea, which was more than the first class appeared to have been given the opportunity to choose.

Once the latter-day liners reached the largest size this class of vessel was ever to attain, it is the quantities of food required for a six-day passage across the Atlantic that appear so staggering. One is reminded of an early concoction of punch given in 1599 by the commander-in-chief of the English navy to his ships' companies. Eighty casks of brandy were used, 9 casks of water, 2,500 large limes, 1,300 pounds of sugar, 5 pounds of nutmeg, 80 pints of lemon juice and a cask of Malaga. To service this to 6,000 sailors, a ship's boy was put afloat on the brew in a boat, and had to be relieved each quarter hour as the rising fumes from this potent little sea overcame him.

For a passage lasting five days, on a ship carrying, say, 2,000 passengers, 75 oxen would be loaded, 25 calves, 110 sheep, 145 lambs, 16,000lb of fish, a high proportion of it lobster and salmon, 4,000 oysters—which works out at only about two oysters per first-class passenger per day—1,000 clams, 350 quail, 120 plover, and snipe, partridge, grouse and pheasant by the several thousand. From the barnyard would be drawn some 4,000 chicken, turkeys and ducks, together with 60,000 eggs. Several hundred wild duck and plover would be on board too, and this is only skimming the cream of the victualling list. To pass a morning, passengers might care to visit the first-class galley and perhaps see row upon row of dishes containing the soufflé mix, ready for the evening ovens.

Wine lists were distinguished on the transatlantic liners, though all suffered uniformly from the fact that the motion of a ship precludes carrying the older red wines. Thus, vintage port was usually unknown. But the wine list for a French Lines ship included 71 champagnes, 8 other sparkling wines, 54 Bordeaux and 48 Burgundies, the latter described by John Mahoney in *The Wine Magazine* as 'a miserable number'; also 2 Moselle, 3 Hocks, 3 Italian wines. The United States Lines were credited with a list that included 81 whiskies, compared with a mere 41 in Cunard ships; but one connoisseur, Mahoney above, placed Cunard at the head of the lines for the variety of their wine lists, and once wrote: 'I felt almost weepy-eyed when I found in a Cunard list a Hambledon white, from Sir Guy Salisbury-Jones's Hampshire vineyard, at 25s.' He was interested, too, in the possibilities of cruising, which must become the most important role for all liners in the future:

> I asked about the type of passenger I was likely to meet, and was told that they varied from bus conductors and charwomen to business and professional couples, retired people, some of the *rentier* class, a few of the landed gentry and probably a burglar or two. These people do not drink wine with every meal...

The luxury liners had a ratio of servers to served of about 1:3, which is comparable with European hotels run in the grand manner. The purely domestic staff in one liner was composed thus: head-waiters, 2; assistant head-waiters, 2; barmen, 6; assistant barmen, 112; stewards, 106; musicians, 11; wardrobe keepers, 3; starchers and ironers, 3; tailor's presser, 1; laundryman, 1; ladies' hairdressers, 2; barbers, 5. This excludes the kitchen staff, an additional 88 members comprising: 1 chef, 1 assistant chef, 31 cooks with an additional 5 pastry cooks, 5 bakers, 5 provision store-keepers, 2 butchers, 1 cellarman and 36 people for washing up. The kitchen staff would alone number much the same as the complement of seamen.

It was statistics of this type which a writer in *Punch* asked for when the first chilly winds were cooling the prosperity of the North Atlantic sea route, and a new Cunarder which was to become the *QE2* was under public discussion. He ended by saying:

> How far will the loaves consumed on one voyage stretch if laid out in a straight line? Can you drive a bus through the funnel?... Somehow all I can visualise so far is that if the pound notes provided by the government to build her were laid end to end they would stretch for 134 miles, 270 yards and 3 inches, or approximately from the Admiralty to Stoke on Trent.

It was then the late 'fifties, some sixty years since luxury had first put to sea, and uneasiness was suddenly being felt about the economics of a route which had hitherto been regarded as gilt-edged. At first, maritime luxury had been the expression of late Victorian, Edwardian and especially transatlantic opulence. When in 1919 the seas were again open for peaceful occasions, it was the age of debunking, with the Bright Young Things as the *avant garde* in a social scene which shook with the new rhythms of jazz. Like so much else that was new, jazz had crossed the North Atlantic from west to east in a liner, but it had been a liner painted for war and carrying amongst the dense crowd of troops occupying the once luxurious spaces, a bandmaster—was it Al Jolson? —with ragtime on his mind. Yet the tone of the Atlantic Ferry when it re-established itself was much what it always had been, its relatively elderly clientele in the first class only remotely acquainted with the Blues as they walked the rooms of the refurbished or new ships in which so much of yesterday had been preserved.

The *Queen Mary* appeared, with seventy-five per cent more space than had that former paragon of luxury, the *Olympic*, and with almost double the gross tonnage of the still highly respected *Aquitania*. Her size, like that of yester-

26

day's *Olympic*, was a cause for wonder. It was pointed out that were the ship put down in the West End of London she would stretch from the Garrick theatre in Charing Cross Road to well down Whitehall, and where she crossed Trafalgar Square the top of the stone cocked-hat of Nelson on his column would be just about level with the boat deck. Why, even the upraised hand of the Statue of Liberty would only just be able to reach the bridge! The *Olympic's* single swimming pool, too, had caused wonder; now it was the *Queen Mary's* eleven lifts. And not one, but three locomotives might have run abreast through any of her three funnels.

Such size brought yet more space for splendours, though this was not the primary reason for it. The simple fact was that it was now technologically possible to produce two ships large and fast enough to run the weekly express Cunard service across the Atlantic, which had hitherto needed three ships, the *Aquitania*, the *Berengaria*, and the faster, less comfortable, but best-loved *Mauretania*.

The years passed, the liners went to war again, and returned once more to the route of gold to find it, amazingly as it appeared to some, golden still. And still to be reckoned with was the attitude of those who had raised startled objections between the wars to the substitution in the public rooms of the *Queen Mary* of artificial flowers for the natural flowers tended hourly by the gardeners. So the services of the latter were resumed at a cost of £650 per voyage. Wealth, if less assured than it had been, less rooted in confidence and custom, was wealth still. In 1957, more passengers crossed the Atlantic by sea than ever before, and the profits of the lines were a comfort. The journal *Shipbuilding and Shipping Record* exclaimed in 1959: 'The western world is becoming richer, not poorer, and there can be little doubt that the sumptuousness of future *Queens* will be as much in demand as now'.

Evidently, it seemed, it was time for a new 'Queen'; already the *Queen Mary* was getting old, now was the time for a similar giantess offering supreme luxury in the first class of a three-class ship. It was time for a new *Olympic*, a grander *Aquitania*, a more splendid *Leviathan;* a new 'Queen', in fact, to cater for the old world ways. But in what manner and to what degree should the new ship do so? This poised subtle questions. Was not the careful segregation of the classes something too well accepted to be abandoned? Would it ever be acceptable that the first-class swimming pool should be overlooked by passengers of the other classes? Was it befitting that the day room for teenage passengers of the first class should be shared by those of the second?

Such questions were many and hard to answer. They still were not answered with assurance when, quite suddenly, it was being found that excellent profits from the ships were becoming merely respectable profits, were becoming slender profits, were becoming losses, and luxury began crossing the Atlantic over an ocean turned into red ink. While the numbers travelling by sea had been climbing steadily during the 'fifties, so had those travelling by air, and even faster. Then the jets arrived, just a dozen years after the *Queen Elizabeth* had made her first commercial voyage and begun a period of such profitable operation. But where now were all the gilded people of yesterday? The answer, of course, was up in the cramped, jammed-full jets eating quick snacks out of plastic cartons—oh, shades of Sir James Charles! A member of the *Queen Elizabeth's* crew spoke of her as a ghost ship whose first-class accommodation you might walk around for ten minutes as she sped along the familiar route, meeting nobody in the tall spreading rooms which had glittered yesterday. And as the *Queen Elizabeth* went one way, she would pass—making the familiar salutations of the sea—the *Queen Mary* going the other, carrying within her expensively-driven hull the great but now un-echoing saloon three decks high.

The last of the enormous liners in the old style was coming into service just before the beginning of the end of the age they sought to extend and maintain in the taste they continued to represent. The *Queen Elizabeth's* first commercial passage was made in 1946, and within two years the President of the United States was observing that this ship and the *Queen Mary* were making between them $50 million a year for Britain. In 1952, the new American liner *United States* appeared, and gained the Blue Riband by crossing the Atlantic in less than three and a half days. An apparent luxury liner, this heavily sub-sidised ship was basically a fast government transport, though her great poten-tial speed and power were kept secret until 1969, when she had joined the outmoded *Queens* and been removed from service. The last of the old-style North Atlantic luxury liners, the *France*, went into service in 1961, just in time for the French Line to regret that they had not planned a smaller and more versatile ship, however much less pleasing to the tastes of those who had heard of the *France* of 1912, the *Ile de France* of 1927, and who had known the superb *Normandie* of 1935, something of whose fine style might be dis-cerned again in the new vessel.

Yet the *France* in her interior arrangement was indicative of the winds of change which her air of very *haute bourgeoisie* might seem to deny. Consider the arrangement of the classes in this ship compared with that usual in the early days of luxury at sea.

The *Aquitania*, when she first came out, carried 750 first-class passengers, 600 in the second class, and between 1,500 and 2,000 in the third, which was occupied by emigrant traffic yet free from quota restrictions. The particularly rich and the particularly poor then made the profits of the ships. By the 'thirties, much of the third-class accommodation had been converted into a class originally heard of when the United States Line had introduced a tourist third class in 1922. Captain Diggle wrote of this class in the *Aquitania* in words appropriate perhaps for the children of the first-class passengers:

> These 'tourist third cabin' visitors have only come to stay in the city during the past two years. They are people who, having heard all about the city afloat, wanted

28

very much to spend a holiday crossing the Atlantic. . . Many of them are clerks who have still their way to make in the world, whilst others are young students and university graduates who find an Atlantic trip a topping way of spending their holiday.

The 'third class' district is at the forward end of the ship. But it must not be imagined that because of its name it is very terrible and dreary. It certainly is not. One would be surprised indeed at the type of people who live in the 'third class' district, and no one need be ashamed of living there.

So the emigrants departed and the tourists, who were about to take over the ships, but not quite yet, were welcomed on board. In 1929 the *Bremen*, of the revived Norddeutscher Lloyd line whose *Kaiser Wilhelm II* had gained the Blue Riband in 1903 with a time of 5 days 15 hours 10 minutes, regained it for Germany with a time of 4 days 14 hours and 30 minutes. A day had been cut off the voyage which Ballin, with his rival line, had shown in the time of the *Kaiser Wilhelm II* should not be shortened but made more enjoyable instead. The *Bremen* carried about 700 in the first class, 600 in the class now called 'tourist', 822 in the third. Then, in 1935, came the French Line's *Normandie* which, had the *France* not appeared in 1961, might have been the final expression of luxury afloat in the sense meant in these pages.

The *Normandie* carried *luxe* and *grande luxe* passengers totalling about sixty, together with 790 first class. There were 654 tourist and 315 third; also a few intermediate classes of small numbers. By the time the *France* appeared more than a quarter of a century later, there were, apart from the *suites de luxe*, only two classes on board, of which 1,500 belonged to the tourist class and 500 to the first. Yet this metamorphosis, compared with the old liners when luxury first went to sea, was not enough. Luxury had to become still more egalitarian, and in the process was transformed into an entirely different commodity.

So came the *Queen Elizabeth 2*, born of many doubts and false starts. We may regard her as the materialisation of the most fully reasoned concept yet as to what a large passenger vessel should be to attract people back to a form of travel no longer indispensable. She is, Jack Newcombe has written, 'a ship boldly conceived by the *Economist* Intelligence Unit, admirably design coordinated by Dennis Lennon, efficiently computerised from engine-room to bakery by Ferranti Argos and impeccably navigated by space satellite. . .'

Just in time, the Cunard backed away from the conception of another ocean transport ferry palatial enough for those who are unable merely to bless their stars and think it luxury. 'The day of the floating palace has been overtaken' declared the London *Daily Telegraph*. Sir Basil Smallpiece, now chairman of Cunard, and guided by the evidence of the Intelligence Unit, said 'In travel, separate class accommodation as a reflection of a hierarchical social structure is clearly out of date'.

Luxury, in fact, was to come home from sea. It had been there for just a little day, between the time when advancing technology had made it possible and society still clung to its older modes and manners; and the time when technology, advancing fast but less confidently, made ocean passenger transport outmoded and society struggled to adapt itself to new modes, new permutations, and manners were with difficulty transforming themselves.

So there is nothing of the Ritz hotels in the *QE 2*. She has the appeal of the best hotel in a seaside resort, one that retains the smartness of being a little less than popularly over-run, though with more emphasis on appeal to youth than such hotels usually offer. Here is a world set afloat of chrome, veneer, brass, stainless steel, and looking-glass by the square yard to show the brave new world to itself, and all done with a taste and imagination that were often lacking in the older, grander ships. Here, too, is a gym, a sauna bath, bingo, floorshows, midnight cabarets, several night clubs. And bars . . . as the advertisements say 'You'll never drink in such a variety of places—and wear out so little shoe leather'. And then there are the launderettes.

The arguments that raged as to whether the ship should have three classes more or less equal in number, or a majority in the tourist third class, with less than a third of the total spread over the first and second, had eventually been decided in favour of a ship carrying only two classes and capable of sailing as a single-class ship. Compared with the *Queen Elizabeth*, the gross tonnage of the *QE 2* is 65,000 as against 83,600, but she carries almost the same number of passengers, has one more deck and three-quarters of the crew.

So luxury for the few is replaced by comfort and fun for the many. It is no more vulgar than the past; it could contrive to be a little less so. However, taste, whether good or less good, can gain nothing by becoming poorer; it may only become less interesting and certainly less entertaining.

But the American who, when writing about the *Queen Elizabeth 2*, described her as taking the sea out of seafaring, was clearly unaware of the background of comfortable ocean travel. Ballin has done precisely this half a century earlier and, to suit his public, had done it more completely. The passengers in the *QE 2* can be, if they wish, in closer touch with the sea over which they are being moved than any former generation in a North Atlantic liner.

Though the deck of a ship at sea can be a place of delight to seamen and landsmen alike in reasonably good weather, and while efforts have been made in the past to bring some element of comfort to the severe promenade decks, the difficulty of reconciling wide, unencumbered deck spaces with ship structures and organisation has usually been insuperable. Well-clothed figures with rug wrappings, artfully situated on deck chairs in the lee of whatever might be available, is the traditional vision of a liner's deck. Besides which, in the earlier days of luxury at sea at least, one sex found neither merit nor pleasure in being scoured by wind or baked by sun. And when the age of sun worship was young and heaven took on the likeness of a lido, still the efforts of ship designers to open out the decks were not brilliantly successful.

In ships confined to the North Atlantic service, the sun may have less appeal than elsewhere, but progressively open deck areas have been spread wider. It is only necessary to compare a liner of such celebrated comfort as the *Aquitania* (1914) with the *Queen Mary* (1936) to appreciate the changing tastes for which the ships were attempting to cater. A successor of the *Queen Mary* and later *Queen Elizabeth*, and the immediate predecessor on the North Atlantic fast service of the *Queen Elizabeth 2*, the *France* (1962) has terraced sheltered decks aft of more generous area than those of her immediate forerunner in the same line, the *Normandie* (1935). In the *Queen Elizabeth 2*, a smaller ship than any of these, the passenger deck space is greater than in any former liner. In stage upon wide-open terraced stage it rises from the extreme stern to the funnel, and then continues beyond, taking in on the way the two open-air swimming pools. Two more pools are below deck, thus far surpassing the old-time wonder of the *Olympic* with her single swimming pool below deck in 1912. The expanses of terraced decks are partly the result of the ship having been designed as a cruising liner as well as an Atlantic ferry, but chiefly they are due to the general taste of today's travelling public. Now the lido has gone to sea, replacing the old, crushed, intimate and draughty decks of the age of luxury.

The liners of that age are now on their way to becoming a memory no less beguiling and imbued with the atmosphere of their period than the Mississippi steamboats with their huge paddle wheels and man high windows, which had preceded them—the steamboats Gothic on 'Ol' Man River'. They were, wrote Lady Emmeline Stuart Wortley in *Travels in the United States*, 'Like moving mountains of light and flame, so brilliantly are these enormous leviathans illuminated outside and inside'.

Peter Newark has described the rococo magnificence of the Mississippi steamboats' interiors: they 'were furnished and fitted at great expense. Inlaid floors, panelled walls, filigree woodwork, stained glass skylights, oil paintings, crystal and gilt chandeliers, vast mirrors; and when the main cabin was set for meals, the finest linen, imported chinaware and gleaming silverware'.

It was the first-class sleeping cabins in these vessels which are said to have first received the name of 'stateroom', later to become familiar in far different ships and before such cabins could justify the inference of the name; had not Dickens been heavily ironical about his 'room of state' in the *Britannia*? The Mississippi steamboats had been running for a third of a century, and were about to disappear for good in the wake of the Civil War, when Dickens sailed to America amid the vigorous discomforts of the first Cunarder. And more than three-quarters of a century was to pass before the new Duchess of Marlborough, the former Consuelo Vanderbilt, made an Atlantic crossing in 1895 that 'was not the luxurious affair' she was to find it in 1953.

Like the ocean-going liners in their turn, the Mississippi craft were displaced by a rival means of transport. For them it was the extending arms of the railroads reaching over the southern states where the prosperous cotton fields spread wide, and the Blues had been born. A new era following the Civil War put an end to steamboat Gothic. Two greater wars were needed to kill the North Atlantic's later version of the paddle-wheel palaces.

The palaces afloat, of the Mississippi first, and later of the North Atlantic, had both sought to banish their respective environments—the one a treacherous river, the other an ocean notorious for its violence. But the banishments could never be complete. Not infrequently a river steamer would become tinder as fire raced through its cargo of cotton and into the splendidly appointed rooms of the first class, which quickly became a charred ruin cooling on the broad, flowing back of the river. The Atlantic, too, as though to discipline an over-confident generation, would from time to time assert its dominion. It did so once in absolute calm. The *Vaterland* had become the *Leviathan*, the *Imperator* the *Berengaria*, and the *Lusitania* was at the bottom of the Irish Sea, when a London first-night audience watched a scene showing the backs of a couple leaning against a ship's rail. Then, breaking their moonlit confidences, they drew apart, to reveal the lifebuoy between them, and the name *Titanic* upon it.

It was a moment of superb theatre. And it expressed the feelings of a generation towards a marine phenomenon which had reached its zenith and was now on the decline as the audience went out into the evening. The liners of the North Atlantic were on their way to join in folklore the steamboats Gothic of the Mississippi.

The future spoke in the *Great Eastern* of 1858

Great Western Steamship Line.

BRISTOL AND NEW YORK.

SOMERSET	..	.. 2000 Tons	..	..	WM. WESTERN, Commander.
CORNWALL	..	.. 2000 ,,	..	..	WM. STAMPER, ,,
GREAT WESTERN	2000 ,,	..	..	S. WINDHAM, ,,
ARRAGON	..	.. 1500 ,,	..	..	GEORGE SYMONS, ,,

The Vessels of this Line carry only a limited number of Passengers, every attention being paid to their comfort and convenience.

RATES OF PASSAGE.

SALOON.—Thirteen Guineas for each Adult; Children under twelve years, 21s. per year; Infants, One Guinea. Return Tickets available for twelve calendar months from date of issue, Twenty Guineas.

These Rates include a liberal Table, without Wines or Liquors, which can be obtained on board.

£5 deposit is required to secure Saloon Berths, the balance to be paid before sailing. No charge for Steward's Fee.

SECOND CABIN Passage to New York, Boston, or Philadelphia, Eight Guineas; Children under eight, half fare; Infants under twelve months, One Guinea.

Second Cabin Passengers are provided with Beds, Bedding, and all necessary Utensils, Wash Basins, &c., and with a good Dietary Table.

STEERAGE Passage to New York. Boston, or Philadelphia, including an abundant supply of cooked Provisions, Five Guineas.

Passengers booked through to all parts of the United States and Canada on very moderate terms.

Twenty Cubic Feet of Luggage will be allowed for each Adult Saloon Passenger, Fifteen Cubic Feet for each Adult Second Cabin, and Ten Feet for each Steerage Passenger free; for all over that quantity a charge of 1s. 6d. for each Cubic Foot will be made.

Goods carried at moderate rates of freight, which may be paid either here or in America. The Shippers to bear all risks of lighterage, river-craft, and fire.

For Freight or Passage apply, in NEW YORK, to W. D. MORGAN, 70, South Street; in HAVRE, to J. M. CURRIE; in BORDEAUX. to CURRIE & CO., 19, Ruy Foy; in LONDON, to DONALD CURRIE & CO., 3 and 4, Fenchurch Street; in MANCHESTER. to W. D.McCALLUM, 14, Tib Lane; in BIRMINGHAM, to LYON & CO., 66, George Street Parade; in HALIFAX, to JOHN EVISON, 40, Commercial Road; in SOUTHAMPTON, to H. MILLER, 34, Oxford Street; in DERBY, to JOHN BRATBY & CO., 27, Bold Lane; in PLYMOUTH, to SANDERS STEVENS & CO., Exchange; and in BRISTOL, to the Managers,

MARK WHITWILL & SON,

GROVE AVENUE, QUEEN SQUARE.

When luxury did not go to sea. In these ships of the Great Western Steamship Line, the steerage fare to the USA was 5gns (£5.25). The saloon, or best, class cost 13gns (£13.65) for an adult, 1gn (£1.05) for infants and 1gn per year of age for children under twelve. In the saloon class the fare included 'a liberal table'. In the second class it was described as 'a good dietary table'

(*Above*) The *Ile de France* was regarded as the supreme expression of French taste at sea, in decoration, furnishing and cuisine, when she made her maiden voyage in June 1927

(*Below*) After the loss of the *Titanic* in 1912, it was left to her sister ship *Olympic*, seen here in drydock for the summer overhaul, to provide the highest degree of luxury in a British transatlantic liner

(*Opposite above*) Arriving on board in 1860; (*below*) 'Good-bye' from Southampton, at about the same date
(*Below*) Passengers on board in the early morning before luxury went to sea
—a sketch by Harry Furniss

(*Opposite above*) On deck in 1891 in the P & O liner ss *Rome* which, in 1903, became one of the earliest cruising liners; (*below*) the promenade deck in the ss *United States*, 53,350 gross tons, in 1953
(*Below*) The promenade deck in the ss *Caledonia*, 7,558 gross tons, in 1894

(Above) An entertainment on board the *Atlantic* in honour of the Great
Exhibition

(Opposite) Passengers exercised on the sun deck of the *Normandie* in the
vicinity of the forward funnel, while dogs were able to exercise in their en-
closed run-around at the base of the after dummy funnel, inside which were
their quarters, at the same elegant level as the suites de luxe

Seventy years before cruising became vital for the economic existence of
liners, the Orient line was advertising a 'pleasure cruise' lasting two months

Comfort on deck in the 1880s

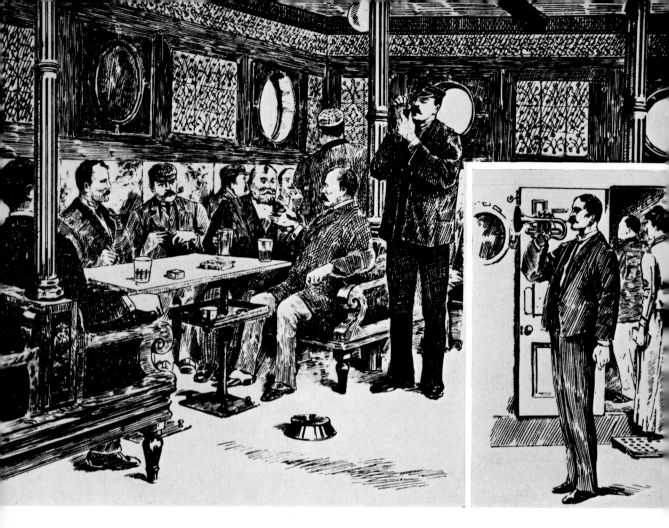

The dinner call in the smoking room

The ladies being dressed . . . for a rough
dinner at sea

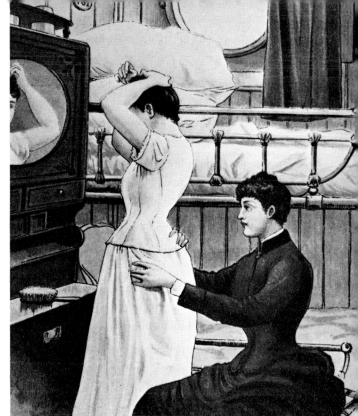

(*Above*) Cricket on board in the 1890s, but no lido deck yet
(*Opposite above*) Deck games; (*below*) some brute comfort but not luxury, represented by Harry Furniss

The *Aquitania*, 45,647 tons gross compared with the 46,439 tons of the *Olympic*, which came out three years later and was her rival in the fierce competition in luxury

The two most important men in
the *Aquitania*: the Captain and
the Head Steward

(*Above*) The main entrance to the promenade deck of the *Queen Elizabeth*
(*Opposite above*) The first-class main hall of the *Queen Elizabeth*, at the top
of the entrance staircase; (*below*) the same, looking the other way

(*Above*) The first-class saloon in the earlier *France* of 1912, a liner whose magnificence made her particularly popular with the French and Americans

(*Opposite*) The *France*: (*above*) staircase to the first-class main hall; (*below*) in the main hall

(Opposite) Victoriana afloat in smaller cabins: *(above)* the *Nahlin*, 1929;
(below) the *Sapphire*, 1912
(Above) Part of the first-class drawing room in the *Queen Mary* as it was
before 1939

(*Above*) First-class reading and writing room in the *France*
(*Opposite*) The *France*: *(above)* in the drawing room of the Gascoigne Suite;
(below) the dining room of a grande luxe suite

(Above) Sitting room in a private suite on board the *United States,* with a mural of curved glass panels by Charles Gilbert, and one of the bedrooms seen through the open door
(Opposite) Two views of the Duck Suite in the *United States*

A bedroom in one of the *United States'* suites, consisting altogether of two bedrooms, sitting room, bath room and trunk room. All the furniture is of light metals and the fabrics are non-inflammable

In contrast with the picture opposite is the older manner of graciousness shown in the stateroom of a suite in the *Aquitania*, where fine woods, cane and fabrics produce a clear fire danger

(*Above*) With *Berengaria* and *Leviathan* on the Atlantic route was the *Ile de France*. She returned to the route after World War II, completely refitted and with one funnel less. Here she is shown leaving for her first voyage after the war, when her competitors were the *Queen Mary* and the *Queen Elizabeth*

(*Opposite*) Rival giants of the inter-war period on the Atlantic: (*above*) the Cunard's *Berengaria*, formerly the Hamburg-Amerika line's *Imperator*, which came out in 1913; (*below*) the United States Line's *Leviathan*, formerly the Hamburg-Amerika Lines *Vaterland* (1914)

(*Above*) A first-class private dining room in the *France*, successor to the *Ile de France* and the yet earlier *France*. The room is reflected in the wall looking-glass
(*Opposite*) First-class staterooms in the *Queen Elizabeth*

First-class staterooms in the *France*

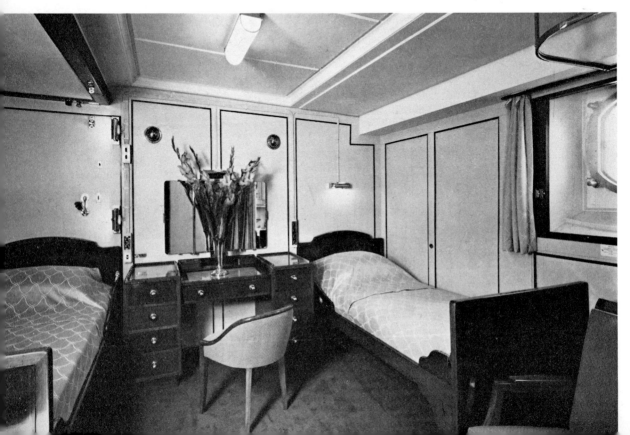

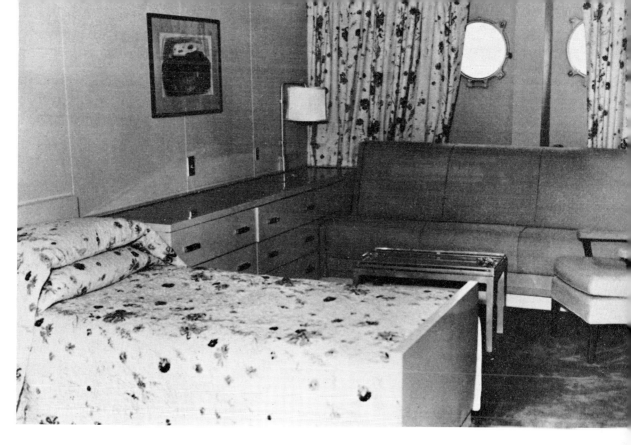

First-class staterooms in the *United States*

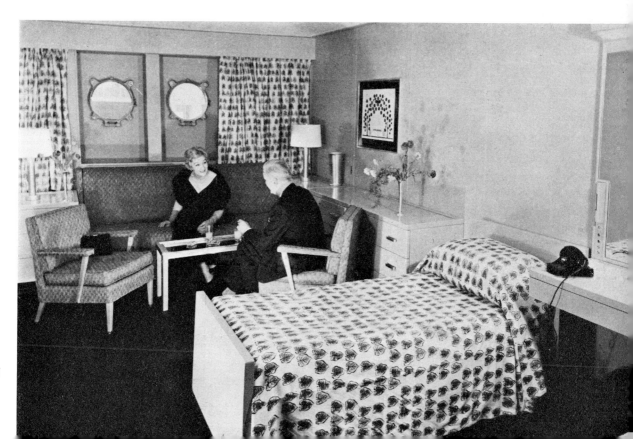

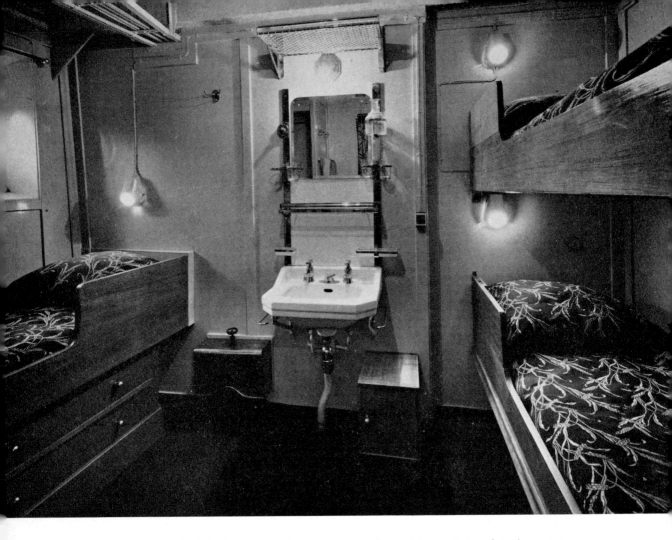

The decidedly modified comforts in the cabin and tourist class staterooms:
(above) the *France; (opposite above and below)* the *United States*

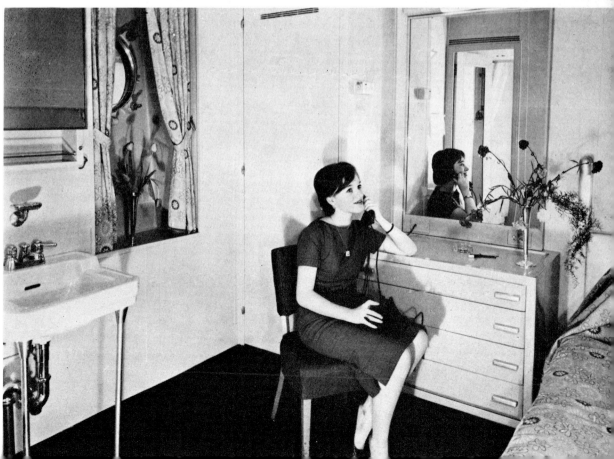

(Opposite) The *Liberté*, originally the Norddeutscher-Lloyd Line's *Europa*, which after reconstruction went into service with the French Line in 1950. The upper picture shows an impression of the ship by the marine artist Marin-Marie; with a slightly different style of painting, the *Liberté* went into service as shown in the lower picture

(Below) The *America*, of 33,500 tons gross, which came out in 1939, was the United States Line's predecessor to the *United States* (p91)

(*Above*) Yesterday's magnificence: the first-class restaurant in the *Queen Mary*

(*Opposite*) First-class dining rooms in (*above*) the *France,* and (*below*) the *United States*

73

Shopping arcades: *(above)* the *Queen Elizabeth*; *(below)* the *France*

(*Above*) In the Ladies Room of the *Ile de France; (below)* a mural in the
hairdressing salon of the *France*

(*Above*) The white and silver Queen's Room in the *QE2*
(*Opposite*) Styles in observation saloons: (*above*) the first-class observation saloon in the *United States*, a room running the breadth of the ship with sixteen full height windows; (*below*) more emphatically a centre for looking out—the *QE2*

(*Above*) The Midship Bar in the *Queen Mary*
(*Opposite above*) The Midship Bar in the *Queen Elizabeth; (below)* alcove
in the cocktail lounge in the *United States*

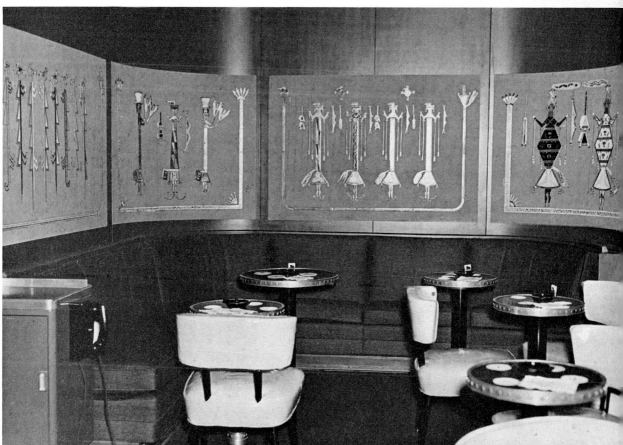

Mid-ocean theatres: *(opposite above)* on board the *France; (oppposite below and this page)* the 352-seat theatre in the *United States*

(*Above*) The Atlantic ferries arrive and depart: the *United States* inshore,
and the *America*
(*Opposite above*) The first-class ballroom in the *United States*. Carved glass
panels by Charles Gilbert, one of which is seen on the left, separate the cocktail bar from the dance floor; (*below*) indoor swimming pool in the *United
States*

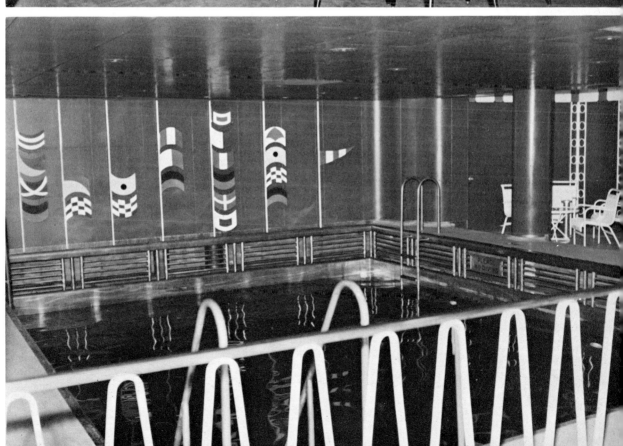

Studies in deck space: *(above)* the limited amount of deck space available in the *Liberté*; *(below)* the more widely spreading areas, and one open-air swimming pool of the *Queen Elizabeth*; *(opposite)* though a smaller ship than the *Queen Elizabeth*, the *QE2* has more deck space and two open-air pools

Studies in the styles of liners: *(opposite)* the *Aquitania,* 45,547 gross tons, of 1914, scrapped in 1950; *(above)* the *Queen Elizabeth* 2 of 1969

(*Above*) The lido deck swimming pool in the *QE2*; (*below*) the Q4 room of the *QE2* by David Hicks, which by day opens on to the swimming pool on deck

Emphasis on youth in the Double Room of the *QE2*, showing what the
designer, John Bannenberg, has described as the 'epic' staircase in aluminium
and steel, and the two levels of the room, which is coloured in reds

(*Above*) The last of her kind: the *France*, still in service in 1970
(*Opposite*) The last two North Atlantic liners in the old tradition of size
and luxury: *(above)* the *United States* (1952), *(below)* the *France* (1961)

Two liners still on the North Atlantic route: *(above)* the *Bremen; (below)*
the *Europa*
(Opposite) The *United States*, withdrawn from service in 1969

ACKNOWLEDGEMENTS

Science Museum, London, 33, 90

National Maritime Museum, 34, 40a, 40b, 41, 47a, 49a, 49b, 75a

Byron & Co, New York, 35a

P & O, 36a, 36b, 37, 38a, 39, 42, 43a, 43b, 44, 45a, 45b, 46, 47b

United States Line, 38b, 58, 59a, 59b, 60, 62b, 67a, 67b, 69a, 69b, 71, 73b, 77a, 79b, 80b, 81, 82, 83a, 83b, 91a, 93

Cunard, 48, 50, 51a, 51b, 55, 61, 62a, 65a, 65b, 72, 74a, 76, 77b, 78, 79a, 84b, 85, 86, 87, 88a, 88b, 89a, 89b

French Line, 52a, 52b, 53, 56, 57a, 57b, 64, 66a, 66b, 68, 70a, 73a, 74b, 75b, 80a, 91b

G. L. Watson & Co, 54a, 54b

Planet News Ltd, 63

Skyfotos, 70b

Tom Molland Ltd, 84a

INDEX

Ships

Figures in italic indicate illustrations

People